Gracie
a rescue dog

Marlene Baird

Copyright© 2022 by Author Marlene Baird

All rights reserved. No part of this book may be reproduced without written permission from the publisher, except by a reviewer who may quote brief passages or reproduce illustrations in a review; nor may any part of this book be reproduced, stored in a retrieval system, or transmitted in any form or by any means electronic, mechanical, photocopying, recording, or other, without written permission from the publisher.

Produced in the United States of America
Authored and Photographed by Marlene Baird
Designed by Eagle Lady Design Studio
Published by Marlene Baird

ISBN 978-0-578-29858-0

Gracie, A Rescue Dog
Available on Amazon.com

Book Stores and Retail Stores:
Order *Gracie* wholesale directly from IngramSpark

Hi, I'm Gracie

For a while I I didn't have a home.
I lived on the street.
So the Humane Society picked me up and was looking after me.

Soon two nice people arrived at the shelter.
They wanted a small dog and I was pretty skinny.
I weighed only 7 lbs. 9 oz.
I went home with them.

It turns out they had quite a few rules for me to learn.

1.
Don't bark at every single noise.

2.
Don't chew on an object just because it is soft.
This was difficult for me because so many things are soft.
Fabric, leather, dog beds…The list goes on and on.

3.
Sometimes a piece of paper falls on the floor.
This does not mean it should be shredded.
This rule also applies to socks.

4.
When other people visit
it is polite to not bark at them.

There are more rules and
I am trying really hard to learn them.

This is the day I left the Humane Society with my new people.
I was kind of scared.

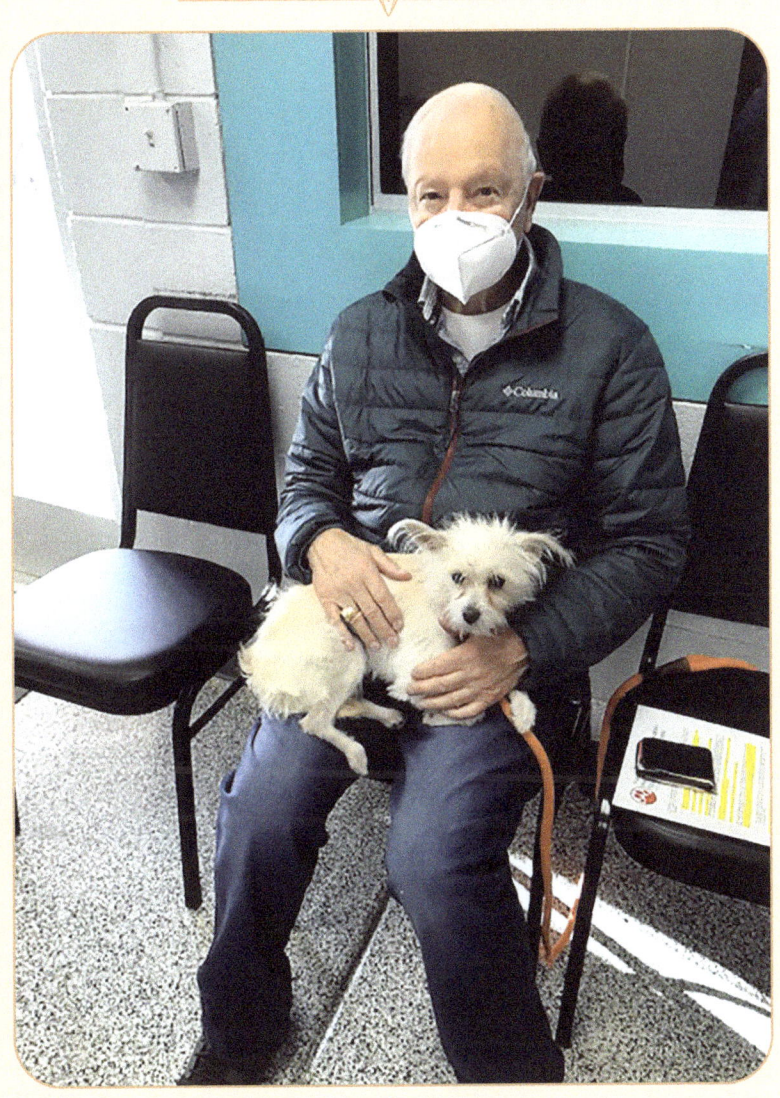

I needed a nap when
I got to my people's place.
They put me on a soft pillow.
It was so nice and quiet.

*In fact, I was so tired
I could sleep anywhere.*

After I was rested up
I began exploring the house.
Apparently that piece of
canvas was a shoe.

I know she's yelling at me but I don't have to watch.

My people bought me lots of toys,
but nothing beats a good chew stick.

I like the sunshine on the deck,
but I forgot my sunglasses.

I did not tear the lining out
from under the love seat.
I was just looking for my ball.

Thanks, Dad, for
such a nice warm bath.

I love a walk, but I thought they only harnessed horses.

This is how you catch moths.

Wanna play with me?
I just killed a brown bear.

If your people like using the computer it is best to have two chairs in the room.

It's good to have friends who visit.

I have chewed up two dog beds, but my nice people bought me another one. I think I will keep it.

I hope all dogs can find nice people to live with.

DEDICATED
to the thousands of
individuals and organizations
across this country
who devote their time,
energy and expertise to
rescue, shelter, foster
and heal helpless animals
so they can find
forever homes.

Lightning Source UK Ltd.
Milton Keynes UK
UKHW051114230622
404851UK00006B/116